BREAKTHROUGH

LEARN HOW THE PRINCIPLES & PHILOSOPHIES OF AN ANCIENT ART CAN BENEFIT EVERY ASPECT OF YOUR LIFE!

PRESTON DUCATI

D1453504

LEGACY PUBLISHING CO.

ACKNOWLEDGMENTS

I would like to thank my children Isabella and Jake for allowing me to love them so much, as their dad! I am extremely grateful for my loving and supportive fiancé, Leah, for staying by my side no matter what life throws at us! As well as a big thank you to all of my friends and family who I am so very fortunate to have around me!

I would like to thank Wang Bo for his friendship, his contribution to this book, and for being one of my inspirations in the Martial Arts!

I would also like to thank my teachers, peers, and students for all their inspiration, support, and commitment to the arts!

TABLE OF CONTENTS

FOREWORD

滴水水穿石石
"Dripping water wears away every stone"
-Chinese Proverb

My story with Preston began 17 years ago at the Shaolin Temple in Shongshan, China, where I had lived and trained since I was eight years old.

At the Temple, we kept a strict schedule every day - we awoke at dawn, meditated, and chanted for an hour, did our morning training exercises, and then ate breakfast, followed by more training, studying, and meditation. As a child, it was hard to stick to this schedule - I found the repetition tiresome, and I was easily distracted. But over time, I came to rely on this schedule to give structure to my life and learning. The discipline of training my body and mind every day allowed me to unlock my full potential as a martial artist, a competitor, and a teacher.

In 2006, Preston was invited to visit the Temple as part of a cultural exchange event. I was honored to host him and his students, and I was impressed with their skill and determination. Even then, I could see that Preston had a strong will and taught his students discipline and perseverance.

I kept in touch with him over the years after his visit and came to know him as a person of integrity with a genuine desire for learning and teaching. When I moved to the US a few years later, Preston was one of the first people I reached out to. He invited me to visit his studios, and we collaborated on some Shaolin seminars. At that time, I was also building my own studio, and I was very impressed with how Preston had grown his business - and even more impressed with the care he showed for his family and friends, including me.

But it hadn't been an easy road for him. He shared with me the personal and professional obstacles he had overcome to find success in his business and his life and how the discipline he learned through martial arts gave him the ability to overcome them.

As a martial artist, breaking through can often mean a decisive physical action - we learn to break through an obstacle with our hands and feet. But even more important is the mental and spiritual strength we learn through practice. We learn to work through pain and uncertainty, try again and again to achieve our goals, and keep setting those goals higher and higher so we can become our best selves.

This book is a powerful reminder that it is not always through swift action that we find success but through perseverance and repetition. Whether the challenge is physical or mental, we need to be ready to face it daily. Remember - true breakthroughs come from within.

Shifu Wang Bo

34th generation Shaolin monk

INTRODUCTION

I am a father, a fiancé, a master teacher in the martial arts, an entrepreneur, a writer, a mentor, an inventor, a hobby musician, and an adventure enthusiast. I believe in living a healthy, well-balanced life. I am a 6th Degree Black Belt in the art of Kenpo karate. I have over 30 years of experience in Martial Arts, safety awareness, self-preservation and escape tactics. I have run, managed, and owned multiple businesses for almost 30 years, and I have trained tens of thousands of people to overcome obstacles in their lives by developing a stronger mind, body, and spirit.

This book is a journey through the principles and philosophies of an ancient art. The topics taught in this book are essential to help preserve our lives, keep our body and mind healthy and robust, and enhance all aspects of our personal and professional lives.

This book is about helping you break through whatever circumstances, people, or events that are in the way of you accomplishing your goals. Realizing that only being "circumstantially committed," limits your ability to keep moving forward towards the attainment of what you want in your life.

Over the years, executives from around the country have hired me to teach the principles in this book. In your hand, you now have those principles. This book is short and sweet. I purposely wrote it that way so that you can read it repeatedly and easily keep learning more from it each time you pick it up.

From Sensei to Student. It's time to begin your Journey...

1

MY STORY

"Everyone is broken by life, but afterwards some
people are stronger in the broken pieces."
-Ernest Hemingway

On Christmas Eve, 1977, when I was five
years old, my siblings and I had chickenpox. Although it was generally a
typical illness for children, something went wrong
with me. I had a terrible headache all day and night,
around midnight, my brother woke up from the
awful noises I was making. He yelled at me to quiet
down, threatening to come over to my bed and

punch me. After several more warnings, he finally got up and marched over to me to deliver on his promise; he noticed something was off with me. Not only was I making weird sounds, but I was also shaking. My behavior freaked him out, and he screamed at the top of his lungs for my mom, who, seconds later, came running into our bedroom to discover that I was having a seizure. She called for an ambulance, and I was taken to the ER of a small, nearby hospital.

After a relatively quick exam, the attending doctor told my mom there was nothing they could do and that I would die. My mom let out a blood-curdling cry and collapsed to the floor (as a father of two children, I can't imagine how devastating it was for her to hear that diagnosis). A moment later, a different doctor came out and said that they were going to have an ambulance take me to Children's Hospital, believing there was a possibility that I could survive. By this time, I was in a coma.

At Children's Hospital, they began running tests on me. My mom called the pastor of our church, and he came to the hospital and prayed with her. Finally, the doctors diagnosed me with encephalitis (inflammation of the brain), an uncommon yet potentially deadly symptom of chickenpox.

As luck would have it, a pediatric surgeon named Dr. James was visiting San Diego from England at the time, lecturing about a new procedure to treat brain inflammation, the very problem threatening my life. Someone at the hospital was able to get Dr. James to come in and perform this procedure on me. It involved drilling a hole in my skull to relieve the pressure, placing a metal "screw" in the opening, and then attaching tubes to it. I remained comatose. My mom stayed at my bedside the entire time, praying for me to get better and talking to me, believing that, somehow, even in a coma, I could hear her voice and want to wake up.

Meanwhile, back at home, my grandfather, who lived in the house next to ours, planted a tree in his yard. It was a Christmas gift from my mom, and he planted it even though a powerful storm was hitting San Diego at that time. My grandpa named the tree Preston and said, "If this tree survives this storm, then so will the boy."

After over 24 hours in a coma, the storm ended. The tree survived, and so did I. The procedure had worked, and I was out of the coma. I stayed at the hospital for another five days of observation. For the next few months, they conducted weekly tests on me. But I had survived.

Still, I was mentally and physically slow for the next several years. School was not easy for me. Focusing was difficult, making reading comprehension, writing, and math difficult. Believing it was a result of everything I'd been through, my mom did not push me to do better in school. As I got older, I knew I had no choice but to work hard to overcome these obstacles.

The tree is still alive and well, and when I visit San Diego, I drive by Grandpa's old house to see it. It acts as a reminder that two of the most essential things in life are time and timing. Not only is time valuable, but we also need to appreciate the importance of timing, for example, the moments when certain people step into or out of our lives or the circumstances in our lives change.

I also learned from this experience that it's important never to allow a loss to prevent you from moving forward. This one experience at a young age could have been extremely harmful to my future. I look at it however, as a positive moment, one that I am thankful for. That moment has shaped the rest of my life and continues to be a reason why whenever I get knocked down (and I do get knocked down), I get right back up with renewed vigor. That is why I don't settle for mediocrity or allow myself to give up on any worthwhile endeavor. It's why I earned my Black Belt but continue working at advancing in the Martial Arts. It's why I keep a consistent workout regimen that continually challenges me and why I own businesses, take on challenges, invent products, and pursue my passions. It's also a big reason why I wrote this book.

We all have stories of negative experiences, no matter who you are or where you came from. We are all faced with adversity at one time or another. The goal is not to let it negatively affect you for too long. It would help if you learned to embrace and acknowledge adversity and move on as quickly as possible while embracing the right lessons from it. The goal is not to let circumstances—whether you have control over them or not— break you and make you want to give up. Don't let your story be your crutch, the reason or excuse why you can't do something. Let it be the reason why you can! What's your story, and how will it serve you to be a positive influence on your life?

We all have struggles, set-backs, and weaknesses, but you are stronger than anything that can get in your way. On the flip side, we all have successes, strengths, and triumphs. No persons story is any more valuable or important than anyone else's. Our personal story helps us develop who we are, our character, beliefs, fears, doubts, confidence, and self-esteem. We learn valuable lessons that inspire, fuel, and help us get back up when we're knocked down, even when it may seem impossible.

Our experiences create our purpose. Growing up watching David Carradine and the movies of Kung Fu Theatre on television inspired me with Martial Arts. The Chuck Norris movies like "Good Guys Wear Black," "An Eye For An Eye," and "Lone Wolf McQuade" also inspired me to set the goal of becoming a Black Belt. This was before I even knew the meaning of the word "goals." I had no sense of what it took to achieve this goal or where it might take me. I had no appreciation of how hard my brain and body would have to work, the years of commitment it would take, and how much focus, perseverance, and grit I'd have to muster to reach this objective. I just knew I needed to do it! Something make-believe had motivated me to push my body and brain further than I ever had since my brain surgery.

I started training in martial arts when I was eight years old, but it didn't last very long since my parents couldn't afford the lessons. It wasn't until I was 17 and working that I could afford classes again.

High school was tough for me, and I came close to not graduating due to bad grades and poor performance in reading and math. However, through my training in the martial arts, identifying, developing, and applying the principles that I have laid out in this book, I learned that I could far exceed my expectations and accomplish things I never thought possible during and especially after I was out of school.

Life throws negative situations and obstacles at us, and it's important to remember that these obstacles are there to help us. We don't always understand or see their purpose at the time, but they are there to create a new path and opportunity for us, and we must accept the changes they will bring.

A few years into my training, after earning my green belt (an intermediate level), I stopped training due to "unavoidable" circumstances in my life. About a month or so later I got a call from my sensei, he asked how I was and if I was ready to get back into the dojo. I realized that my situation was still ongoing and that stopping my training did not stop my "unavoidable" circumstance. So, I got my butt back in the dojo. A valuable lesson I learned about letting circumstances get in the way of achieving my goals. To this day, I'm thankful he made that call. There are many stories like this in my life, as there probably are in yours. There are people in your life that helped you get back on track. Maybe it was just a nudge, or perhaps it was a big push. Be thankful you have these people in your life. Just make sure you tell them from time to time how grateful you are for them being in your life.

This is a book about the principles and philosophies that I've acquired through many years of successes and failures. This book is about screwing up, failing, and getting back up. This is a book about grit and not giving up. It's about learning to pick yourself up off the mat and live a life that does not beat you down.

This is over thirty years of martial arts practice on paper, covering philosophies and principles about physical, mental, and emotional well-being, awareness, self-preservation techniques, and daily disciplines. It's about building a healthy relationship with yourself so that you can have a more beneficial relationship with anything or anyone. Let it help you break through circumstances and not give up when you are after something you truly desire. Most importantly, this book gives you the tools to experience a healthy, complete, and well-balanced life you love.

Live your life with purpose and never settle for just getting by. Show up as the best "you" for your community, family, friends, and life. Know your story and be thankful for it, whether joyous or painful. Life lessons are everywhere, especially underneath the negative bad experiences. It's through our reactions to those negative experiences that we either rise above or don't.

Remember: Your weaknesses can become your strengths! Your spirit is your root, grounding, and overall internal makeup. A strong spirit keeps your mind and body strong. By learning to turn our weaknesses into our strengths, our spiritual roots grow stronger.

This book will cover the importance of proper breathing, exercise, relationship building, and challenging your mind, body, and emotions. We will also dive into the mental and physical elements of awareness and personal safety.

"If you don't know yourself, you lose 100% of the time."
—Ancient Samurai Proverb

The goal is to continuously work on your strengths while doing the work of turning your weaknesses into strengths. Review your strengths and weaknesses, belief systems, and overall physical, mental, emotional, and spiritual health. Live in a mindset of continuous improvement, taking small steps over time. First and foremost, when taking stock of where you stand, be honest with yourself. Lying to yourself does you no good.

. . .

What's your story?

Make a list of your weaknesses.

Make a list of your strengths.

What are some of the ideas from this chapter that you can apply to your personal life?

What ideas from this chapter can you apply to your professional life?

"If this tree survives this storm, then so will the boy."

This is a current photo of the tree that represented a promise of life from my Grandfather.

2

BREAKING THROUGH

"It ain't about how hard you hit. It's about how hard
you can get hit and how much you can take and
keep moving forward. That's how winning is done!"
-Rocky Balboa

On a hot blacktop pavement in Orange
County, California, I tested for my
black belt on November 5th, 1994. The
test was a grueling 8 ½ hours long. It took everything
I had physically and mentally to see it through to the
end. As the day wore on, I collected bruises from
strikes meant to test whether I was physically strong
enough. This was in addition to enduring the intimi-

dation techniques of instructors wanting to see whether I was mentally strong. Midway through, I could feel the aches and pains from hours martial arts practice, calisthenics, and the weight of my thick canvas martial arts uniform that had grown heavy with sweat. At the end of the day, I achieved my 1st Degree Black Belt, also called "Shodan."

Toughness has two components: mental toughness and physical toughness. Physical toughness can get you far, but mental toughness will keep you going when physical toughness wants you to quit.

The ability to focus your energy and mindset beyond or through an obstacle or circumstance you may face, to endure especially when it gets difficult, requires practice.

Imagine for a moment, you are learning a technique that requires you to break through a board or a brick. Initially, fear or doubt might kick in, and on your first attempt, you might hold back and not succeed in breaking through the object. Then a coach teaches you to think differently about your energy and the object you are striking. You are asked to imagine going through the object as if you were doing nothing more than pushing your hand through a bucket of water. You take a few focused breaths and imagine going through the object. Then you open your eyes, and BAM! You smash through the object! Did you get stronger in the short time between the first and second attempts? Of course not. Adjusting your mindset made all the difference. Many things in life are like this.

What are some obstacles in your life that could use a mindset adjustment?

How can you look at them differently to make adjustments?

You may constantly struggle in certain areas, but that's not a reason to give up. Change is never easy, but it is necessary for growth. Change requires not only stepping out of your comfort zone but also finding a deep-rooted reason that your life demands the change, and this root needs to be strong enough that nothing can sabotage it.

Bruce Lee said, *"Notice that the stiffest tree is most easily cracked, while the bamboo or willow survives by bending in the wind."*

Mindfulness is about being aware and conscious in the present moment, mentally, physically, emotionally, and spiritually. To start this process, take a few deep, slow breaths for a count of four seconds before breathing out for six to eight seconds. During this exercise, your eyes can be open or closed, and you don't need to be in a completely quiet space. Put down the book for a moment and practice this a few times. You will use this and other breathing practices from this book throughout your journey and, more importantly, as a daily practice routine to benefit your mind and body.

"It's ok to lose to an opponent, not ok to lose to fear!" — Mr. Miyagi

Learning how to breathe and focus on the outcome you desire is a powerful tool to help you combat fear. Everyone has fears that present themselves in our personal and professional lives. It can be fear of success, failure, or even fear of someone trying to hurt you physically. You will be tested daily, sometimes less, sometimes more. At the end of each day, you should ask yourself: Did I give up, or did I keep going?

Bruce Lee said, *"Don't fear failure. Not failure, but low aim is the crime. In great attempts, it is glorious even to fail."*

Many great achievements are often preceded by many failures. The faith and belief in your endeavor's worthiness must be more powerful than the doubt or fear that will get inside your mind. Train your mind to move forward from any circumstance in or out of your control. There may be times when this seems impossible. Giving up, however, will only make ultimate failure your reality. Luckily, you can fail and keep going as long as you're willing to get back up!

Fear, doubt, uncertainty, lack of confidence, or self-esteem can keep you down. You must break through these barriers and keep going, without giving up, for continued self-improvement.

Write down one step you can take right now, to begin this journey.

Now that you have identified that one step. Break down that action into smaller acts that you can take within the next 24 hours.

Once you've taken these small steps, you're going to start to feel a sense of accomplishment. It's time to start adding to your list. What's the next step to tackle?

For example, during my black belt test, I wanted to give up many times. In business, there have been many times that I've also wanted to give up. However, I've always known that not quitting would benefit me more than giving up. If you want to start your own business, start researching what is required to take that first step in your business endeavor. If you want to get in better shape, start walking daily and keeping a closer eye on what you eat. The vital piece of this is to understand that you must start with something, no matter how small. Success builds confidence. The act of starting will inspire you to take more steps toward growth.

Change is a series of small daily disciplines that build up over time and bring you closer to your desired goals. This is why it's crucial at the beginning of your journey to take on the mindset of improving in small steps.

When taking these small steps, we must be diligent in practicing strong character, putting forth our best effort in what we do, demonstrating sincerity to others and ourselves, and establishing a strong sense of mental, emotional, and physical self-control. Displaying kindness and compassion and reminding ourselves that we are not entitled to anything in life is also crucial.

We put forth our best selves to help bring out the best in others. Be humble and respect others and yourself.

Have the discipline to keep growing as a role model and good citizen in your community.

"I live my life by two words: Tenacity and Gratitude. Tenacity will get me where I want to go, and gratitude will not let me be focused on being angry or negative along the way." —Henry Winkler

I keep a coin in my pocket, wherever I go, that says, "Whatever It Takes!" This is my reminder to live each day with tenacity and to push through adversity.

In my other pocket, I keep a rock that my daughter gave me. This is my reminder to live each day with gratitude and to focus on the good in the world around me.

Every morning and night, whether I've had a good or bad day, I hold the coin and rock in my hands and remind myself of the importance of living with tenacity and gratitude. You're going to have bad days, and it's essential to keep focusing on your tenacity and gratitude. What ideals inspire you in your life? Identify your ideals, find something that keeps you reminded of them daily and continue to live your life by them. A large part of breaking through circumstantial commitment is not giving up because of people, events, and circumstances. We will discuss this more in the next chapter.

I am excited to be on this journey with you, exploring how the principles and philosophies of an ancient art can be applied to all areas of your personal and professional life.

Ralph Waldo Emerson said, *"Life is a journey, not a destination."*

Reading a great book or attending a great seminar does not change your life if it does not connect with you mentally and spiritually. Everyone will take different lessons from this book. The goal here is to get you to seize life at this moment and not allow negative circumstances to get in your way. Therefore, it's crucial to be in the right frame of mind from the start, so you are ready to acquire and accept the instruction and information and then take the action needed to go after what you desire. Remember, it starts with small steps, and we continue to build on them from this day forward. Rome was not built in a day, and the same can be said when accomplishing any worthwhile goal.

When you are learning, be learning, and when you are leading, be leading. In martial arts, I teach our instructors that when they are in their own training class, they are to put on—figuratively speaking—their student belt. They should put on their instructor belt when they are on the floor in a teaching role.

"Look in the mirror as the mirror reflects only one thing —the truth."—A saying from one of my Kenpo teachers many years ago.

What ideas from this chapter can you apply to your personal life?

What ideas from this chapter can you apply to your professional life?

3

WHAT IS CIRCUMSTANTIAL COMMITMENT?

"We must be ever ready to move in our lives, and not become too comfortable in one state for too long. When we become complacent, we stop growing."
-Kenyo Furuya

I am a father, fiancé, teacher, entrepreneur, writer, mentor, musician, inventor, and adventure enthusiast, who currently holds the honorable rank of 6-degree black belt in the art of Kenpo karate. I continually seek new physical and mental challenges for myself, not wasting an opportunity to learn and grow. My life revolves around spending time with family, surrounding myself with meaningful relationships, working hard, staying focused on my profession and projects, and taking time to experience the culture and experiences surrounding me. I have run, managed, and owned multiple businesses for almost 30 years, and I've trained tens of thousands of people to overcome obstacles in their lives by developing a stronger mind, body, and spirit. Through my teaching, I show how the principles and philosophies of an ancient art can not only help preserve life and keep your body and mind healthy and strong but can also enhance all aspects of your personal and professional situations.

Over the years, men and women from around the country have hired me to teach the principles in this book. One exercise I conduct with these groups has them breaking boards with their bare hands to allow them to see how they can break through that one barrier in their lives that might be holding them back. I show them how they can crush any goal and achieve that next level as effortlessly as they've smashed through the board. I have to admit, even after all this time, witnessing this is an exhilarating experience.

. . .

What is Circumstantial Commitment?

I grew up without a father. My dad left when I was one year old. Grade school wasn't easy for me. I was a scrawny kid who got picked on and bullied. Then in my 20s and 30s, I had many failed relationships, including a tough divorce. At age 44, I was financially ruined.

From every one of the adverse circumstances listed above—and many others that I haven't detailed—I learned how to rebuild, strengthen my confidence and belief in myself, and become stronger.

Circumstantial commitment means staying committed to any worthwhile goal or endeavor and not letting circumstances in or out of your control stop you from continuing on your journey. It is about knowing where you are going and not letting anyone or anything stop you.

The mission will always stay the same no matter the circumstance that enters your path. Imagine driving somewhere, and you encounter a blocked road. Do you turn around and head home or search for an alternate route? Life has its way of constantly throwing roadblocks at us. Our response should not be to give up and go home but to find a way to continue moving toward our goal.

I am a martial artist for many reasons, one being that I don't like bullies! When we think about a bully, there are many images that may come to mind. A tough guy picking on a smaller guy, or a boss taking advantage of her position, but sometimes circumstances or events can also act like a bully. This can be a key factor to not being circumstantially committed in your life, in other words, not allowing circumstances to dictate your path, is to not let the bully win!

What circumstances do you believe are getting in your way?

But, maybe, you're the obstacle.

Life may teach us humility, but we should also see that we are extraordinary beings capable of amazing things. The human mind is an incredibly powerful tool. You could lose everything tangible in your life, but no person or thing can take away your spirit, tenacity, love, passion, gratitude, or mind. You have the power to withstand and rebuild from any negative circumstance that comes your way. Don't let any past negative experiences hold you back from the positive experiences in your present and future.

What situations from your past could be holding you back?

You are not only responsible for the actions you take in response to circumstances that are in your control. You are also responsible for how you respond to circumstances that may be out of your control.

Challenge yourself to look at a recent negative experience and identify how it could lead to growth for you.

What's a recent negative circumstance that was out of your control?

What's something positive you might learn from this experience?

What ideas from this chapter can you apply to your personal life?

What ideas from this chapter can you apply to your professional life?

4

WHAT WILL NOT GET IN YOUR WAY AFTER TODAY?

"When you lose, don't lose the lesson."

-The Dalai Lama

The ability to make decisions. This is what separates us, humans, from the rest of the animal kingdom.

Deciding how we treat ourselves and those around us. Choosing how we begin our day. Deciding how to respond to people, events, and circumstances that come our way. Determining the nature of our true mission.

This ability, however, is not enough to put any decision into action, and actions are what help us grow, improve, and move past our current situation. Action inspires perseverance, dedication, motivation, and a deep-rooted goal that cannot and will not be broken no matter what gets in your way. This deep root will take over once your motivation is exhausted.

Live a life of purpose - on purpose!

Be deliberate in your actions!

Motivation alone will not be enough to push you forward on your journey. You must have a reason or desire that is stronger than motivation so that when you get knocked down, you will have a rationale to stand back up and keep going.

Because one thing is certain: You will get knocked down. It doesn't matter what the circumstance is. It could be something as minor as a broken shoelace that knocks you down or pulls you off your path or it could be something as large as a natural disaster. Or anything in between.

Get in the habit of regularly saying to yourself, *"Nothing can stop me unless I let it stop me."* Be in the mindset of pushing through no matter what gets in your way. We call this the "Warrior Spirit!"

With the Warrior Spirit, you will still face moments of uncertainty, doubt, fear, and other negative emotions, but they will not stay long. They will be temporary visitors that your warrior spirit will send away because it knows that the longer they stay, the more they will negatively affect your life and those closest to you. Staying in a negative mindset robs you of the ability to see the good around you and positive opportunities hiding in plain sight.

What you say to yourself regularly matters. Your internal voice can be an excellent tool in developing the very best in you. Here's an example of practicing your inner voice: *"I can and will make it through anything that tries to knock me down or defeat me! I have a Warrior Spirit inside me, and no person or thing can take it away. I understand that each day is a test of this Warrior Spirit. People, events, and circumstances will constantly challenge my Warrior Spirit, but they will fail every time because my Warrior Spirit is unbreakable, unstoppable, and will never give up."*

Come up with your own mantra. Say it often, so it is an available resource in those moments when you need to push through adversity.

Find a physical test that challenges you to push past what you thought possible. Doing a difficult physical challenge can build confidence and strong character. When times get tough, you should be able to look back on that accomplishment and know that if you can do that, you can get through anything that comes your way. Examples of physical challenges can be signing up for a bike ride, run, or obstacle event. It could be getting up every morning with a brief stretching or calisthenics routine or a daily push-up or plank challenge. You can get a friend or significant other to join you for this workout routine, so you are accountable to each other. What do you have to lose? Go for it. Break through your comfort zone. Start small, but start! Accept your challenge today.

What ideas from this chapter can you apply to your personal life?

What ideas from this chapter can you apply to your professional life?

5

LIVING A HEALTHY AND BALANCED LIFE

"To keep the body in good health is a duty...
Otherwise, we shall not be able to keep our mind
strong and clear."
-Buddha

We live in a fast-paced world, where our devices can consume us if we allow them to. Being available to anyone at all times is not always a good thing. A cutoff switch is crucial. The mentality of extreme working has turned worse since Covid-19 hit our world. Working from home has blurred the lines between work and home, between our business and our personal lives.

When you leave work for the day, you need to feel as though you are mentally leaving it. Having an "off" switch from work is essential. Employees across every industry have burned out because they lack this off-switch. Those emails will still be there tomorrow. That memo will still need to be written the next time you log in. Part of my role as a mentor is to help teach people how to achieve balance in their lives. Reaching a perfect balance is impossible. Life is always leaning just a little too much to one side because it constantly shifts. Part of learning balance, however, is recognizing when the balance is off and knowing how to make adjustments so that our work, family, and personal lives do not bleed into one another.

We get a surge of dopamine and serotonin when checking emails, texts, and social media, and our devices can become addictions. They add to the problem of blurring the lines between work and personal time. While it is important to stay informed, it's also important to find a balance between these devices—especially social media—and your life.

When you wake up in the morning, don't be so quick to reach for your phone. Practice waiting 30 minutes or an hour before you pick it up. Instead, first look at your goals for the day, hydrate, stretch, workout, or just sit for a few minutes and find gratitude for what you have in your life. Waking up like this is much healthier for you mentally and physically. Take the time to do this. The body and mind need these small moments to help replenish your energy.

Separate personal and business emails, so you don't get sucked into work every time you check your messages. Turn off email, social media, and other notifications on your phone. Turn off your ringer at night, and keep your phone out of your room, so you don't feel the need to reach for it in the middle of the night. Practice being in the moment. Do not let yourself get lost in other things when you are hard at a task. For example, if you are with your family, be with your family mentally, physically, and emotionally. The same is true for your hobbies, friends, work, etc. This is called "seizing life at the moment." This is not easy to do regularly, and you won't ever be perfect at it, but just like anything else worthwhile, it requires regular practice and small steps to become more proficient.

. . .

Three areas to start focusing on today:

1. Regular Healthy Food

Good food is paramount to a healthy lifestyle. You need the right energy to take on life. Stop consistently putting food into your body that does not help you be the best person you can be physically, mentally, and emotionally for yourself and those around you. Be mindful of what kinds of foods and how much of them you are putting into your body.

Every morning my fiancé makes us coffee, and I make us a protein smoothie filled with greens like kale or spinach, protein powder, Greek yogurt or peanut butter, cinnamon, banana, blueberries or marionberries or strawberries, and flax seeds or chia seeds. On the weekends, I eat two fried eggs with bacon or sausage and sometimes avocado toast. For lunch, I have a meal delivery service that brings me a nice mix of proteins and veggies daily. I put an ice block in a small canvas cooler bag with my meals if I have a long day ahead, two protein bars, and an apple or dark chocolate-covered almonds. I also have a large water bottle that goes with me every day to get enough water, about 70-90 ounces. Since I'm on the go a lot, I don't want to be in a position to have to search for healthy food, especially when I get hungry. This is an easy way to eat well for lunch, and most meal delivery services deliver a week of yummy fresh meals for under $12 a day. For dinner, we mostly cook meals like stir-fry with chicken and veggies, chicken or turkey, and a salad.

Coming from an Italian family, I do love fresh pasta. I grew up living next door to my grandparents from Italy. My grandma (Nonna) would make everything from scratch. I was a lucky kid growing up being able to eat fresh pasta and pizza; my favorite was gnocchi. My family and I sometimes like to do that, when we have the time. Like most of us, we don't always have that kind of time, so we buy fresh pasta and enjoy it without having to spend so much time making it from scratch. My teenage daughter is a vegetarian and loves to cook, so we occasionally make vegetarian meals together. I also enjoy a cocktail or two with dinner or after dinner. The point is to find some foods you like that are also healthier for you. Create a plan to start being more aware of what you're putting in your body.

Stay away from soda, eat less sugar and bread, and get more protein along with healthy fats and carbohydrates in your diet. This doesn't mean that you have to give up all the foods that you love; it does mean that you should identify the foods that fall into those unhealthy categories and monitor how much of them you are regularly consuming.

Cooking at home more often, using fresh foods, and eating out less often is a great way to start this process. Also, it's fun to learn to cook your own meals. Stir-frying with veggies, chicken, steak, or tofu is a great way to start learning your way around a kitchen. It's easy to make, tastes great, and is suitable for you.

Use the 80/20 rule regarding food, meaning 80% good food and 20% whatever you crave. Start with a 60/40 ratio before building yourself up to 80/20. Research some recipes that sound easy and are healthier than eating out. Get your partner involved, you can make cooking together a fun learning experience. Good food will give you the fuel your body craves.

2. Regular Physical Exercise as a Healthy Outlet

Most mornings, I get up and hit the gym I have set up in my garage to get my warm-up, workout, and stretch in for the day. I have a large blackboard with my workouts written up, so I keep myself accountable. I put on my headphones and get mentally and physically in my zone. The mornings I do not hit the garage gym; I practice Martial Arts, mountain biking, hiking, or something that helps keep me mobile and keeps up my strength, coordination, balance, and range of motion. I update my workouts and continually work on challenging myself because I know that doing this will benefit me mentally, physically, emotionally, and in every other area of my life. This helps me show up as my best to my family, work, friends, and life! When I speak with people about the subject of health and fitness, it does not seem to be as much of a priority in most people's life as it should be. Don't wait to start a workout routine. Start something today. Start with a daily 20-minute walk. Start small if you must, and gradually increase the intensity.

Being the owner of your body's health is something nobody else will do for you. Taking care of this "earth suit" you were given is your responsibility. Having a healthy outlet is good for your mind, body, and emotions. Take a little time each day to enjoy that physical and mental outlet. You'll thank yourself.

Examples of how you can take care of your body include martial arts, hiking, biking, skiing, snowboarding, surfing, climbing, running, yoga, tennis, basketball, meditation, gardening, weightlifting, walking, or anything else that gets your body moving. To start your workout journey, find something you enjoy and build from it. Have a mindset of continuous small steps of learning and improving!

3. Healthy and Meaningful Relationships

In a moment of contemplation, in my early 40s, after many failed relationships, I took some time off and went on a soul-searching mission. My goal was to write down what I wanted in a relationship, being very specific with every detail. I wrote down everything that I wanted and everything I did not want in and from a relationship. I also had to look in the mirror and be honest with myself about what changes I had to make to be the best man I could be for that person I wanted to find. I had a former student that was the head chef for a beautiful hotel in Kauai; what a perfect place to go on my mission. I spent each day writing, surfing, running, kayaking, hiking, and enjoying my chef friends' amazing food. Within two months after my trip, I met the woman with all the qualities I wanted and none of the qualities I didn't. It's truly amazing how a list, a goal, or anything you want out of life in any area can come into your existence by writing it down, believing you deserve it and letting it be a regular focus throughout your day. See what you can do by putting this into practice in your life, and it doesn't take a trip to Kauai to make it happen, although it certainly doesn't hurt either.

Identify what you want, write it down, believe you will find it and have the humility to change. This will help give you more of what you want and less of what you don't.

Those closest to you see the best and worst of you. A healthy relationship with family and friends is important for a well-balanced life. Your partner and children will need you to show your best self as much as possible—your best listening, understanding, compassion, physical, mental, and emotional you. It is all about daily practice. No one is perfect, and you will screw up from time to time. It's ok to show emotion; emotions are a part of each of us. When we identify them, we can control them. Know the triggers that set you off and get you frustrated, so you don't get lost in them.

"Emotions go on and on when fueled with words"
— Buddhist Proverb

Be the first to improve your relationships, and don't expect someone else to take the lead. Relying on the other person will push improvement further away.

Trust is paramount to a healthy relationship with yourself and others. Everything is built on trust.

Ultimately, be happy with yourself and for yourself. No one can make you happy. Other people can only enhance your happiness. With this understanding, you will be in a better position to love yourself and your partner.

Write down your weaknesses in any of these three areas:

- Healthy Food
- Regular Physical Exercise

- Healthy and Meaningful Relationship

Where can I improve?

Don't take for granted the importance of the support of family and friends when attempting to improve these three areas of your life. Life is too short to spend time with people who do not support your passions. Alternatively, it is equally important to support the people in your life. Support does not mean always agreeing with people or liking the same things. It means being there for one other. It can mean just being present to sometimes listen or to offer advice when asked for it. In unhealthy relationships, people use each other to escape their problems. In healthy relationships, the parties acknowledge and address each other's problems and support one another.

Family, friends, co-workers, and significant others cannot stop you from accomplishing your goals, but realize that they can sabotage them, even unintentionally. You must develop good communication with those closest to you, so they do not get jealous or voice negativity about your true mission and goals. Be excited to share your passions with those you love. Be confident. Be bold. How you bring up these goals to others and respond to their comments is important. If they have concerns, don't get upset or angry or assume it means that they don't support you. Ask more questions, uncover more information, or share your thoughts and goals in greater detail rather than just sharing the desired outcome. Leave nothing important unsaid.

We live in a world of computers, cell phones, and social media. Take the time to unplug and connect with those closest to you through more intimate forms of communication. Look each other in the eyes, talk, and connect face-to-face. This type of communication is an art that, if not maintained, can be lost and harm even the healthiest relationships. Pick up the phone or visit the people who are important to you. Take those small steps that let them know how much you appreciate, love, and value them in your life. Keep your relationships current. If they are in your household, don't assume they know how you feel or how much you love them. Express it through actions and words. Don't wait until you're at someone's funeral to articulate how much you appreciated that person in their lifetime. Go tell them now!

What is something you want to accomplish but are afraid others will consider overly ambitious? Do you know how to take that first step?

What ideas from this chapter can you apply to your personal life?

What ideas from this chapter can you apply to your professional life?

6

SOME DAILY DISCIPLINES OF AWARENESS TO PUT INTO PRACTICE

"We don't rise to the level of our expectations; we fall
to the level of our training."
-Archilochus

I n my life, I've had to use martial arts to
protect my loved ones or myself. I use the
principles and philosophies of the art almost
daily when dealing with situations involving business, family, or friends. I occasionally use it to calm
down strangers and prevent problems from turning
dangerous. One of the most critical elements of
mastering my skill sets is staying in control and not
having to use them. It's about not allowing a situa-

tion to get out of hand even if the other person wants to escalate the matter.

I've only physically fought when there was no other option but to fight. I admit that it felt good to have the skills to be in control mentally and physically under tremendous stress. Staying in control is rare for people put under higher-than-normal pressure. People will often see red and lose control of their minds and bodies. We all have a beast inside of us. We can either pretend this beast does not exist or take steps to understand it, learn how to control it, and have it work in our favor if we ever need it.

The same goes for using weapons of any kind. We live in a society that does not usually teach respect and understanding of dangerous things like weapons. Instead, they are feared and talked about as bad. While it is critical to understand the extreme danger of a weapon in the wrong hands, it is also critical to learn how to respect weapons. You are more likely not to misuse them if you understand them. Know that you will only bring a weapon out if you need it to protect yourself, your loved ones, or someone who cannot defend themself. Generally speaking, people properly trained with a particular weapon are not the ones committing the crimes because they understand the needed respect and control that goes along with anything that can be considered dangerous.

During extreme times of stress, like a dangerous situation where self-defense is required, breathing is crucial to helping you quickly decide on the best course of action. By getting in a regular practice of being aware and in control of your breath, you are better prepared for a variety of circumstances that may come your way.

Throughout any given day, you will experience stress, anger, sadness, feelings of being overwhelmed, anxiety, and countless other negative emotions. It's not only important to have proper breathing practices when we feel relaxed, it is imperative that our breathing be steady and controlled during our most emotional and stressful times. Regular, proper breathing is also good for your overall health. Make a small goal to practice daily the breathing practices I have covered earlier in this book.

I recently coached a woman with thousands of Instagram followers on awareness and self-preservation. She had reached out to me because she was involved in a stalker situation. After we'd had only a couple of sessions, she was at a park working out when a car pulled up close to her. The man in the car rolled down his window to say something to her. His demeanor seemed threatening. Right away, she noticed his mannerisms and possibly his intentions were not friendly and before he could say a word, she shouted, "No, I'm not interested!" in a strong direct voice. This was awesome, especially since she is normally a sweet, kind, and polite person. He quickly drove away from her and did not return; a potentially dangerous situation was avoided.

While being kind to people is a beautiful characteristic, it is also imperative to follow your instinct and to trust your gut. Listen to your instinctual feelings, and you will know when to say yes and when to say no.

The Importance of Awareness:

We see it every day. When we are in our car or a store of any kind, we see it in shopping malls or when we're just walking down the street, whether in a small town or a major downtown city. People wearing headphones, their faces buried in their cell phones or other electronic devices, hoodies over their heads, or walking while staring at the ground with a slumped-over posture. What I'm talking about are people who walk around unaware. This includes everyone from young children to older adults.

Electronics distract people, especially cell phones, which allow people to unplug when overwhelmed or stressed mentally. These devices contribute to being completely unaware at the moment to such a degree that they are oblivious to other people or events happening around them.

A disease is spreading in our communities; it is a lack of awareness. I call it *"the death of awareness."*

In stores, shoppers with their carts clog the aisles as they stop to send off a text. Even people who aren't on their phones seem unaware of their surroundings like they live in a fog. They congregate in the middle of a sidewalk unaware they are blocking fellow pedestrians from walking. Drivers are also often oblivious, failing to use turn signals, stopping at green lights, or, with their heads down, staring into their phones as they wait for the light to change. With the rapidly advancing technology at our fingertips, this problem will only get worse unless we teach awareness to our children and the people in our communities.

We can all agree that this problem of people lacking awareness has gotten out of hand. People are oblivious to the good and bad people that surround them.

Unfortunately, criminals are taking advantage of this growing problem of obliviousness. We are making it way too easy for them to do their job.

My mission is to teach, coach, and inspire the people in our communities to stop this unnecessary obliviousness by learning and applying awareness principles so they can pay it forward and pass on this valuable information to family, neighbors, coworkers, and friends.

Knowledge is power!

Daily Disciplines of Awareness to Put into Practice:

It's been said that we don't rise to the level of our expectations; we fall to the level of our training. You can't be prepared for everything. However, you can practice some simple daily disciplines to greatly help prevent you or your loved ones from becoming a victim. You do this by recognizing potentially dangerous situations and knowing how to respond appropriately.

1. Eat something every 2-3 hours and drink enough water throughout the day. A lack of nourishment and de-hydration can cause unneeded stress and a short fuse. Don't get in the habit of being "hangry." This is not a good recipe for dealing with a variety of situations. Keep water and snacks in your car, backpack, purse, briefcase, office, etc.

2. When driving, if you are stopped at a light or in traffic, give enough room between you and the car in front of you, enough so you can see their back tires touching the pavement. This gives you a path out in an emergency.

3. Keep doors locked when driving or stopped. If your car does not have a setting to do this automatically, practice doing it yourself every time you get in the car until it becomes routine.

4. Do not let your gas tank go below 1/4 full. This allows you to drive your car a reasonable distance in an emergency, whether it's getting to a safe area,

escaping trouble, or getting someone to the hospital. Stopping for gas in these situations is not an option.

5. While walking, keep your chin up and shoulders back, maintaining good posture. Use your eyes and notice the people around you, their actions, and the baseline, meaning the current state of the area you occupy. Is it quiet? Is it loud? How are people acting? If you know the current baseline, then you will also know when it changes. Then if it does change, you can respond quickly. Being a hero does not always mean handling a dangerous situation alone. It means deciding on the best response for the specific situation. This could mean getting out so you can get help, like calling 911 or asking a stranger for assistance.

6. Know your exits when you are out and about, especially in a mall, hotel, restaurant, school, church, or any indoor place where people congregate. Get your family or the people accompanying you involved in a game where you practice this type of thinking. Under stress, you will not only recognize that a decision needs to be made, but you will be able to take concrete actions to keep yourself and your loved ones safe.

7. Practice your breathing, which is a powerful tool. Safety is not about finding a big solution to a situation immediately. Instead, it's about starting with small steps, and you need proper breathing to do this. Set up a daily meditation practice for yourself. A few minutes of daily meditation will provide a variety of excellent benefits. There are many types of meditation practices. Do some research to find the one that best suits you.

Breathing = Thought. Breathing = Action. Breathing = Power.

My everyday carry:

- Pocket knife
- Tactical pen
- Flashlight

Remember, you must train with anything you decide to carry for self-defense purposes. Otherwise, you will be unable to effectively use the weapon when needed. Or worse, it might be used against you.

· · ·

What are some of the ideas from this chapter that you can apply to your daily routines?

What ideas from this chapter can you apply to your personal life?

What ideas from this chapter can you apply to your professional life?

7

EXPERIENCES AND VALUABLE LESSONS LEARNED

"Life is a journey, not a destination."

-Ralph Waldo Emerson

In my life I've experienced sky diving, bungee jumping, paragliding, scuba diving, surfing, kayaking, paddle boarding, water skiing, wakeboarding, wakeskating, snowboarding, rappelling, zip-lining, hiking, biking, motorcycling; owning my dream car—a Maserati; driving a Lotus around a race track; buying homes; living in San Diego; living in Hollywood and Beverly Hills; living in Seattle; owning businesses; dining at the finest restaurants;

eating the very best steak; drinking the finest wine, scotch, whisky, and craft cocktails; drinking Hawaiian moonshine; smoking the very best Cuban cigars; meeting and training movie stars and famous musicians; traveling to China, Italy, France, Bora Bora, the Hawaiian Islands, Canada, Mexico, and Alaska; taking many flights and road trips across the U.S.; seeing many of the 50 states and amazing sights of this beautiful country; riding a Harley to Glacier National Park in Montana, around the Hawaiian Islands and along the west coast of California. I went to see the Jazz Festival in New Orleans; appeared on TV; played in a few bands, singing and playing bass guitar and acoustic guitar on stage to songs I wrote; visited the Shaolin Temple in China, training and fighting in that temple; achieved a 6th-degree master-level black belt in Kenpo karate; and much more!

This is a list I have added to over the years, and I will continue to do so since learning and growing should be a regular occurrence in a well-lived life.

What I've learned in no particular order...

I've learned that life is a wild adventure mixed with the good, the bad, and the ugly. But, overall, life is wonderful.

I've learned that giving up is not an option.

I've learned that being an adult means being strong and being able to face adversity and how to keep moving forward.

I've learned to be patient and how every day is a test of this lesson.

I've learned that I never thought I could love two little people so much, my children, the loves of my life, Isabella and Jake.

I've learned that most people are good and mean well, and will pull together if needed.

I've learned that experiences, large or small, are more important than just having stuff.

I've learned that no matter how many ways I've learned to harm, there are always more ways to help.

I've learned that although every day I am tested, every day is different and that every day I must improve, grow, and learn.

I've learned that the most valuable part of getting knocked down physically, mentally, or emotionally is getting back up.

I've learned that there are people that will let you down. But there will also always be people that have your back.

I've learned that children can empower you and make you stronger, but they can also bring out your greatest weaknesses, which I work on improving every day.

I've learned that I most often get what I need. I am blessed to have great experiences, situations, and people around me.

I've learned that feeling good and laughing regularly will help keep your mind and body happy and healthy.

I've learned that growing up is not easy and that everyone needs a connection to something bigger than themselves. Mine was the martial arts.

I've learned that playing lawn darts, pretending to be a stunt man, and building unstable bike jumps, along with many of the other games I played as a kid, was probably not the safest way to spend my days. I hurt myself at times, but it was a lot of fun and helped make me who I am today.

I've learned that playing football and other rough sports with my older brother and his friends can cause pain and injury, but it also makes you stronger.

I've learned that every time I try to use the restroom on a plane, we hit turbulence.

I've learned that you must embrace the suck.

I've learned that I can take a hard punch and give one as well.

I've learned that growing older should mean you have a greater understanding of taking care of your mind and body, and not the other way around.

I've learned that life is a game. In games, sometimes you lose, and sometimes you win, but whatever the result, it does not mean you stop playing.

I've learned that whatever job you do, big or small, no matter the pay, do it well.

I've learned to be good to others, open doors, say please and thank you, check in on others, and be sincere and authentic.

I've learned that loving what you do is more important than money; if you love what you do and put in the work, the money is guaranteed to come.

I've learned that everyone has had a tough time in some way growing up. Whatever our circumstances were in the past, we are in control, as adults, of what comes next.

I've learned that giving back feels incredible, whether in small or large amounts.

I've learned that we do have a choice in how we respond. Circumstances might not be our fault, but they do become ours to deal with.

I've learned that learning, in and of itself, is an important task every day.

I've learned that even though my children are young, there is so much I can learn from them as an adult.

I've learned that clear communication will help avoid many potential problems on the horizon.

I've learned that there is a difference between reacting and responding. When dealing with a non-violent situation, don't be so quick to react. Take a few seconds to absorb what is being said and respond appropriately.

I've learned that it's vital in life to love what you do as your profession and to be in relationships that support and enhance your happiness and help you grow. Have good friends that inspire you, too.

I've learned that a good healthy, well-balanced, loving, passionate relationship without drama is possible. However, you must know what you want in a person and what you don't want.

I've learned not to mistake plastic for cash.

I've learned that some of the most challenging times of my life sometimes turn out to be the most motivating. Similarly, there are positive times that up end up being demotivating.

I've learned not to be a victim. Trust your instincts.

I've learned it's ok to say "no" to people, circumstances, and events in your life.

I've learned there is an important difference between living a life with awareness and safety or living a life full of paranoia and letting fears or fear of others dictate your life.

I've learned that respect is more important than popularity.

I've learned that all experiences, good or bad, put me right where I need to be in my life. I am very thankful for all I get to experience.

I've learned it's important to have your place of Zen where you can go from time to time to help put life in perspective, a place where you can get away, even if it's for a brief moment.

I've learned the importance of having a daily reverence.

I've learned that when people are only circumstantially committed, they often veer off their path to success.

You have abundant opportunities in your life. You have skill sets, people, and circumstances around you to help you become and achieve what you desire. The goal here is to recognize opportunities, be ready for them, and invite them into your life so you can take action. Once you decide what you want and take action to get it, do not let anyone or any circumstance get in your way. Live your life committed to what you set out to do, and let that commitment be stronger than anyone or anything that could come your way.

Thank you for sharing your time with me. It's been a pleasure to accompany you on your journey. I wish you the very best along each step you take in your worthwhile endeavor. Remember, never give up! Continually strive to become healthier and stronger. Live your life with deliberate purpose. Be grateful daily and live with tenacity and gratitude.

Even if you only learned a handful of helpful words of wisdom from this book, it may just be the pieces missing from the puzzle of your life.

It takes a village for us to achieve anything in our lives. Never forget who's been there in your life to help you during the hard times.

Together We Are Strong!

As Sitting Bull said, *"As individual fingers, we can easily be broken, but all together, we make a strong fist."*

I wish you the very best in health, strength, happiness, and safety.

.　.　.

Be Strong, Be Bold, Stay Focused, and GO *Breakthrough!*

Put together your own list of what you've learned in your life and add to it from time to time...

What are some of the ideas from the chapter that you can apply to your personal life?

What are some of the ideas from this chapter you can apply to your professional life?

8

STICKING TO YOUR NEW HABITS

"As long as you got a fist and you keep pushing it forward, you're going to knock something down."
-Sylvester Stallone

There are many ideas in this and other books that you read that you will want to get started on right away. This excitement makes you want to get lots done quickly. However, remember that any actual change takes a plan. New habits take time, dedication, and consistency. They also take small steps to create. If you try and do too much at once, then you will likely burn out and quit, don't do that. Pick one of the habits in this book, practice it, work at it, strengthen it, and then add to it. Set goals to start the next habit once you have an understanding of a plan and consistency of application of the first habit. If you forget or get sidetracked and miss a day, don't stop and assume you cannot change. Get back up, BREAKTHROUGH, and keep going. As mentioned previously; everyone fails a few or many times before accomplishing their goals, don't be the one that stops just before you are about to receive what you desire.

Whether your goal is small or large, when you fail, remember that it is only a step in your journey, not the end. A journey is a continuous set of steps you always grow and learn from. Failure is not your end game; you have more in you. Believe this, know this, live this. Change your mindset on what failure means, and make it something you learn from, adjust, and grow from. Not something that beats you down and makes you feel insecure or unable to keep moving forward. You are stronger than that, so go show failure who you are, and don't back down.

Go Breakthrough! Stay Strong and Healthy!

CONCLUSION

LESSONS FOR MY CHILDREN

"To the world, you may be one person, but to one
person you may be the world."

-Dr. Seuss

Dear Children, I am your father, teacher,
guide, mentor, and protector. You are the
love of my life. Take your time to grow
up. Stay innocent, stay sweet, and stay loving. Trust,
believe, play, laugh, sing, dance, and be inspired in
each moment. When you are an adult, you'll see that
the world can be cold and brutal. Even so, there will
always be love, even when you think there is not.
There will always be good, even when sometimes all

you think you can see is evil. There will always be happiness within and around you, even when all you feel is sadness, anger, or other negative emotions. Be strong even through pain, hurt or fear. This will help keep you mentally strong. You will laugh, cry, and want to scream, but always know that it's ok to express your emotions. Do not keep them locked up. But, also, don't let these emotions control you. Embrace these feelings. Let them be there for a short time, then take a deep breath and move on.

Be grateful for what you have, and don't be upset about what you do not. Take care of yourself, laugh at yourself, love yourself, and be yourself. Treat your mind and body well. Be responsible and accountable for everything you do. Remember that no one thing, person, or event can take you away from what you desire in your life. Don't let anyone tell you that you can't accomplish something; if they try, prove them wrong. You will meet those people that make you doubt yourself, your ability, and your mission in life but do not let them. You are far stronger than you know, and this knowledge will keep you strong through adversity. It's ok to be afraid. You just can't show it all the time. You will make mistakes and fail often, but these are the stepping stones to your success. They are there to teach you how to get back up, keep going, and never give up. Love your life, love yourself. Be grateful, loving, strong, compassionate, honest, and courageous. Never expect anyone else to be your happiness. Others can make you smile and laugh and give you many other positive emotions, but only you can make yourself happy.

Live, Dream, Love, & Appreciate Life.

-Dad

What would you write in a letter to a loved one?

ABOUT THE AUTHOR

 Preston Ducati is a martial artist of 30+ years who shares insight and understanding of how principles and philosophies behind an ancient art can enhance your personal and professional life. He holds the rank of 6th degree Black Belt in Kenpo Karate and is continuing to work towards his 7th degree Black Belt. He helps people break through the obstacles in their life that are keeping them from accomplishing their goals. He keeps it simple for the reader to apply and discusses essential topics such as awareness, safety, and meditation.

He was financially ruined at age 44 and can teach you how to get back up after being knocked down mentally, physically, or emotionally.

He has run multiple businesses over the past 25 years and shares this powerful knowledge with the reader. Over the years, executives from around the country have hired him to teach the principles in this book.

He also runs seminars and consulting to continue the processes taught in this book.

Preston currently resides in Seattle, WA. If you are interested in getting more info about upcoming seminars or booking a consultation to see how he can enhance your professional or personal life, you can reach him at the information below.

Email: breakthroughbook@prestonducati.com

Website: prestonducati.com

Made in USA - North Chelmsford, MA
1354139_9780996666084
01.18.2023 0846